SPACES:
HOW TO FIND PERSONAL PEACE

WRITTEN BY:

DR. NEENAH BOYD, PHD-HNSD

AND

MINISTER TAMYKA RAMSEY-GORDON

Read about how Mitchell and Lucille found spaces to allow self-love and self-friendship blossum as cells in their bodies as their romance took several turns and struggles. They ultimately found personal peace and the end of loneliness and sleeplessness.

Publisher's Name: Dr Neenah Boyd, PhD-HNsD

ISBN: 978-1-968442-34-7

Table of Contents

ABOUT THE BOOK:

Sleepless nights can make a person feel lonely. Loneliness can cause a person to have sleepless nights. Both can cause one to have a reduced quality of life. In this book we will handle each condition both separately and at times together. Both conditions can stem from many causes that may be physical, mental, psychological, neurological, or a lifestyle, to name a few. It is the intention of the primary author to look at the whole person, in a holistic way. This book seeks to help those who cannot get enough deep sleep at night or who communicate very little with other people, during the course of their day. We want the reader to benefit from this book. Or the reader can pass the book's information along to a loved one that suffers from loneliness and/or sleeplessness. It is hoped that after reading this book, the reader or the reader's loved one, can enjoy restful days where they no longer fall asleep unexpectedly during waking hours. And we want the reader or the reader's loved one, to feel like a well-liked individual who is a part of a vibrant society, conversing with others and no longer feeling that tinge of rejection that often accompanies loneliness. Reading "SPACES" will take the reader to spaces in their mentality where peace can be found, leaving the reader in a better space. Thus, the name of this book, "SPACES."

ABOUT THE AUTHORS:

This self-help inspirational book has entertaining drama woven within the scholarly content. The drama narratives which convey examples of the scholarly content are written by the skillful co-author who flourishes in the performing arts as well as the literary arts. The co-author volunteers as a literacy educator, has a career in the healthcare sector, and is the daughter of the primary author. She is proficient on the piano, drums, xylophone and began lessons on the violin in grade school. She began Suzuki piano lessons at age six. She is an Ordained Minister. Her prose and poetry have been published. She enjoys writing about love. The co-author also enjoys creating abstract artwork, interior designing, and photography. She has acting and voiceover experience and has done comedy and impressions. This book also draws upon the depth of knowledge and wisdom of the primary author who is a deep thinker with a high IQ and the ability to distinguish divine inspiration. The primary author is a retired school-based Speech/Language Pathologist and has formal education and degrees in Education, Communication Sciences and Disorders, theology, and the new field of neurospirituology. She has Master's degree medicalspeech/language theory and medical speech/language therapy experience in a hospital. The primary author has business experience as the CEO/Chief Financial Officer/Founder of a small nonprofit humanitarian organization that promoted and distributed a unique Holocaust DVD of a friend who was a survivor who experienced unlikely Nazi leadership that saved his life. She produced the video. Her PhD-HNsD is a cross between a spiritual degree in theology and neurospirituology which studies what goes on spiritually in the synapses between nerve impulses as it applies to how we communicate in prayer, in our private thoughts, and when we communicate with each other. Her heavy concentration

and birthright in Judaism study, diligent Torah observance of the 613 commandments with alacrity in the Orthodox Chassidic manner and customs practice, undergirds much of her being. It attributes to her high EQ, emotional calmness and ability to calm others. Her compassionate Christian upbringing and Christian Counseling training, contribute to her high EQ, emotional quotient, that is higher than her very high IQ of 152, but has been said to be "down to earth." Her IQ was tested with an IQ test at age 11. It was suggested that she be in MENSA, the high IQ society. She was placed in an isolated scholars class for kids with high IQs, from the 7th grade on into high school. She made her living as a speech/language pathologist in the schools. Serving ages preschool to high school, Jr High was her niche, probably owing to the fact that her fun years were in Jr High during her formative years.

Though she had a love for children, she excelled at the Master's degree level in the area of adult acquired Central Nervous System communication problems, like Parkinson's Disease and Dementia. She was and is gifted with God-given revelations in her career as a communication sciences speech & language pathologist andneurospirituologist. She is the author of "QUOTES PLUS: A BOOK OF QUOTES & THOUGHTS OF A DEEP THINKER PLUS TRUE SHORT STORIES." She is of German, Irish, and Native American Indian Cherokee heritage, with beautiful brown skin.

INTENT OF THE BOOK:

As the title implies, it is the authors' intent to present information that may combat two ills that plague people --- loneliness and sleeplessness. By reading this book, a deeper look at and understanding of how the sciences of communication skills and the combined workings of our nervous system and the spiritual impact of living our lives with the best lifestyle as we can, may enable the reader to take positive action to hopefully find personal peace and get rid of loneliness and/or sleeplessness in themselves or can help the reader help their loved ones who may not be living their desired quality of life.

The primary author implies the prospect of cells and spaces in the body that can be activated at certain stages in life to ensure and promote healthy sleep and social interaction.

CHAPTER 1

ZYGOTE ENERGY

First they made love. Zygote energy was exploded. They were married but acted like new lovers who found themselves in each other's arms dying to go all the way!!

They never had a church wedding nor any ceremony of any sort. But they had been married for 37 years...united by God with the Heavenly Host as their witnesses and audience. Mitchell & Lucille vowed to spend Eternity together.

CHAPTER 2

Deep Thoughts on ZYGOTE ENERGY:

Zygote energy can be explained in two ways. First, a zygote could be the prenatal development in a pregnant woman. Second, it could be in the mind of a person who is "pregnant" with a fantastic idea. Either way, a zygote begins with fertilization. The sperm fertilizes the egg and the beginnings of a baby person is called a zygote. Later, an embryo is developed, then a fetus, then at full term the mother and father go into the delivery room of a hospital, and a child is born.

Or in the case of the person who wants to birth a money-making idea, first it is conceived in spiritual fertile ground. Then it grows, takes shape, and is delivered to an audience of one or however many people want to hear the whole idea.

Zygote energy is just a poetic way to say that in the introductory story, the couple's juices were strong and flowing.

CHAPTER 3

COLORADO HAVEN

The fictional story of the love birds, Lucille & Mitchell continues here:

The next day found the couple in their living room in the city they have lived in for the past 12 years called, Colorado Haven.

"I told him, go and call your brother, effective immediately. And tell him to make way. The city is coming to ruin."

The crops were gathered at the gate but Acropolis began to eat them one by one. "Wow! Makes for an intriguing catch phrase in a detailed tale that could be the talk of the town," thought Lucille!! She imagined this to be the opening of the next novel she wants to write.

It got cold in the mountains of Colorado and even in the well-known Shenandoah Valley that everyone in the town frequents. Mitchell had taken the horse to the barn at sundown and was going back to the cabin to keep his wife warm by the fireplace that he had just gotten started half past the hour. It looked like the snow was coming sooner than expected. Lucille, his wife, had washed and folded several blankets in preparation for the storm. They were going to have a romantic evening and she had apple cider brewing. They even had marshmallows for roasting by the fireplace.

Mitchell enters their home (cabin) and says to Lucille, "I can't find my chain saw." Lucille says, "Well, when Uncle Drew came by, he asked to borrow it. I didn't think you would miss it."

Mitchell responded, "It's not going to be much use. I have to take it to Middleton for repair."

"Well, don't you worry your man hands about that now. You come in here and get this hot cider I made for you, while we lay." Lucille replied.

Lucille wrote fiction novels to alleviate any strain. Mitchell and Lucille's two kids were 21 and 22 years of age and they were grown and were on their own, away from home. So consequently, Mitchell and Lucille were capturing the love of their youth. Passion and erotic behaviors were the norm now.

"Yeah, I guess a little cider won't hurt a hard-working man like me!" said Mitchell.

Mitchell took off his coat and all the winter clothes he had on. Lucille was looking at all her husband's finely designed muscles. Oh Lord, you have blessed me! Why do I deserve a man who is so refined?" Lucille thought.

Lucille had a white lace southern bell mini skirt dress on to spice up the moment. But while Mitchell's back was turned while he was taking off his clothes, she managed to quickly take her dress off and all you could see was the perfect elevated position of her beautiful big round and full breasts. Mitchell always thought he was the luckiest man in Colorado Haven to be blessed with a woman whose breasts were that perky and perfect even after two, I said two not one…wonderful kids.

Mitchell turned to her and said, "mmmh you can make me get a hard-on so quickly, you pretty southern bell."

"Now why you wanna make a shy girl like me blush like that?" Lucille cooed sheepishly. Lucille began to rub Mitchell's back and started to kiss him slowly. He gently turned around and began mouthing her big succulent breasts. "Oh! You make me so excited…" he whispered.

They both started breathing and panting kind of on the heavy side. "Oh let me rub your fanny, Cille". The steam was on! "Yes Mitchell! I give myself to you" she said. He licked her thighs and kissed them inch by inch gently. He enters. "Ohhhh! Make love to me Mitchell and oh don't you stop, my Romeo!!"

Well, it turns out the night was long and seemed endless. In and out, up and down, God was smiling on them. Boom! They explode and ignite together! Zygote energy! "Whoooah! I'm tired," Lucille exasperated. "Me too!" Mitchell chimed.

"Let's eat these marshmallows and turn in for the night. We have a long day ahead of us tomorrow." "Yeah, and I gotta get my chain saw."

"And I have to write this novel." They both smiled and went to bed……………………………..

Lucille remembers that evening in Colorado Haven like it was yesterday. But now she is alone and lonely. No Mitchell around, and the adult children rarely talk to her. And it's been a long time since she's gotten a good night's sleep, a problem that has returned. She remembers the days of sleeplessness in the early years of her relationship with Mitchell. Lucille had moved back to her hometown in North Carolina. She remembers their youth when Mitchell had a big surprise for her.

CHAPTER 4

THE BEGINNING OF LUCILLE AND HER BIG SURPRISE

"Half past the hour and I'm still not out of the house! Come on Lucille, you can do this!" Lucille exclaimed. Talk about incitement. This was Lucille and Mitchell's second Valentine's Day and he told her to dress up---he had a surprise for her.

CHAPTER 5

DEEP THOUGHTS on THE BEGINNING OF LUCILLE AND HER SURPRISE:

Incited excitement during the day, if the person is not brought down off of cloud nine, it can lead to a sleepless night. Too much excitement on a steady basis can be detrimental to a person's sleep hygiene. In the same way, the repeated successes in one's life can leave them waking up with only 3-4 hours of sleep, only to find it hard to go back to sleep.

There is hope for people who suffer this way. As the Bible never explicitly dictates that we get 8 hours of sleep a night, I believe that adults do not have to be that stringently consistent to have optimal sleep hygiene. Studying with medical doctor internalist & neurosurgeon and theological philosopher G. D. Carmile, MD, PhD-HNsD at the G. D. Carmile Private School of Theology & Philosophy revealed that four nights of 8 hours of sleep is probably enough for a week for 3 weeks of the month for the average adult healthy needs. Many factors go into the amount of sleep the body will take to replenish our vitality. Though the amount of activity during the day that a person exerts has an effect on the amount of sleep that the body will seize, this is not always the case and it is not always consistent throughout the week and month. Because the body is a precision machine that works in concert with many health factors, the average body will "take" the amount of sleep that it divinely needs each night…as if sleep is a part of, or the final stage of digestion. After all, lots of animals like the lion sleep after they eat. Some humans do so too. Mothers know that a good way to get an agitated baby at night to fall asleep, is to put a little bit of oatmeal in their bottle. However, we as humans can interrupt this orchestrated action by our willfulness.

Once the cycle of sleep/wake is disrupted, it is necessary to employ all of our faculties to restore healthy balance, known here as homeostasis.

Let's take a look at a working dictionary definition of what "sleep" is as a noun. Sleep is "a condition of body and mind that typically recurs for several hours every night, in which the nervous system is relatively inactive, the eyes closed, the postural muscles relaxed, and consciousness practically suspended."

It is my thought to approach the answer to sleeplessness with a look at the whole body…a holistic approach that encompasses the physical, mental, psychological, and spiritual.

Let's also look at the stages of sleep, specifically, "Entering Sleep". The following is an excerpt of an article from www. verywellhealth.com.

"Entering Sleep"

Using an electroencephalogram (EEG), a non-invasive test that records brain activity, scientists are able to see how the brain engages in various mental activities as a person falls and is asleep.

During the earliest phases of sleep, you are still relatively awake and alert. At this time, the brain produces what are known as beta waves— small and fast brainwaves that mean the brain is active and engaged.

As the brain begins to relax and slow down, it lights up with alpha waves. During this transition into deep sleep, you may experience strange and vivid sensations, known as hypnagogic hallucinations.

Common examples of this phenomenon include the sensation of falling or of hearing someone call your name.

There's also the myoclonic jerk; if you have ever been startled suddenly for seemingly no reason at all, then you have experienced this."

DEEP THOUGHTS continued. ANALYSIS

Sparks and flirtatious love remarks and actions, have a total body effect on a married couple. Both the co-author and primary author of this book are married to very loving men. Beyond that, the primary senior-age author has had a pronounced self-loved and self- friendship since the age of 12, with no codependences ever, owing to a healthy parental example of a couple in love who gave their three daughters, and no sons, an abundance of security, and middle upper middle-class upbringing though they were minorities.

Though the primary author has a well-managed lifestyle of healthy eating and exercise, she attributes her sleep habits and people connectedness to her love for herself. The primary author's husband feels blessed to be married to her. The coauthor, growing up with this self-loved, self-friendship mother, ended up marrying a man who loves himself, is a friend to himself, and loves her with unconditional love, like her mother. Love nourishes. Love heals. Love cures. Love and self-friendship are key.

Entering sleep can often be the chief problem of those who experience sleep deprivation on a rather regular basis. This may be Lucille's problem in our drama. Let's see about her and her "SURPRISE!"

CHAPTER 6

CONTINUATION of LUCILLE AND HER BIG SURPRISE

The fictional story of the love birds, Lucille & Mitchell continues here:

Now Lucille and Mitchell had been dating for about a year and two months. The infectiously close couple loved each other much and they both knew their relationship was serious. Mitchell is a health and fitness nutritionist. He also teaches an aerobics class at the local health club, which coincidentally is on the same block as the restaurant they are meeting at tonight. Lucille speaks four different fluent languages. She is a foreign affairs court translator. She had Valentine's Day off and assured her boyfriend Mitch, she would be there on time and READY! Wedding bells...well of course she thought of it but they never really talked too much about it for any extended length of time. Nonetheless, they both affirmed each other. They would definitely have to pray on such a big decision.

"Spaghetti straps! Check! 6-inch heels! Check! Alright, he's going to love it! I'm out the door!"

Now at this point, Lucille is flying down the freeway to meet the love of her life...praying the whole way there that she can make it. Her cell phone rings and it's Mitch.

"Where are you, baby?" Mitchell questions.

"I'm on West Ridge about to pull over. My car is about to stop. I'm out of gas. Mitch, Bae, I'm sorry I'm late." Lucille said frantically.

"Just hang tight Cille. Are you at West Ridge and Palm, near the trestle?"

"Yes." Lucille answered.

"Ok I'll take care of the car. I'll be there in five minutes."

"Ok, thank you Boo. I love you." she spoke.

"Love you too!" he replied.

Lucille pulls into a parking lot by the trestle and prays and waits---patiently. Thank God it was a sunny 60 degrees February day in North Carolina. So as Lucille waits, she's not too uncomfortable. For 30 seconds her eyes are closed while praying but when she opens them, she sees a clean silver brand new Mazda 6000 with a Big Red bow on it driving into the parking lot. From a distance she wants to think that it's Mitch but no, this was too good to be true. Finally, her eyes make the visual connection that it is Mitch coming to her rescue driving a brand-new car. What a surprise!

They both step out of their cars and Mitch says, "This is your Valentine's Day gift, Baby!" Lucille jumps into his arms and squeezes him very tightly and kisses him. "I can't believe it! Thank you, Boo! This is perfect timing too!" she says with excitement.

"I'm going to have your other car towed to the gas station and I'll drive it to the restaurant, because little do you know, the surprises have just begun………………..." Mitch explained.

The evening proceeded to be magical! When Lucille got home and laid in the bed to go to sleep, she thought, "Oh my goodness, have I truly met my Prince Charming? He came to my rescue, and more!" That night, Lucille had extreme difficulty falling asleep. This was becoming a regular occurrence, especially since things were also going so well with her job and her siblings.

CHAPTER 7

DEEP THOUGHTS on THE CONTINUATION OF LUCILLE AND HER BIG SURPRISE:

As stated earlier, incited excitement during the day, if the person is not brought down off of cloud nine, can lead to a sleepless night. In the same way, the repeated successes in one's life can leave them waking up with only 3-4 hours of sleep, only to find it hard to go back to sleep.

Studying with George David Carmile, MD, PhD-HNsD revealed that many successful individuals do not keep regular sleep hours. However, this can take years off of their lifespan. This would be because of a kind of "stress" that could be considered, "good stress". The term "eustress" is used for this type of stress. The word "euphoria" may come to mind when you see "eustress". A Merriam-Webster dictionary definition of "eustress" as a noun is, "a positive form of stress having a beneficial effect on health, motivation, performance, and emotional well-being".

What can we do when we find ourselves lying awake in bed at 2:00a.m.? If it is because of eustress, we can first, recognize it as such. Then we can see it as the zygote energy of chapters 1 & 2 that is keeping us awake. Perhaps we've been impregnated with a marvelous idea. We should get up and write our thoughts down and let the idea develop. In this way, we are finishing the "digestion" of the day as we ruminate and reflect on the positive things of the day. Or perhaps we are stirred by a way to solve a nagging issue we or a loved one is experiencing. Whatever the case, we should not react with alarm nor disgust that we are losing sleep. We can simply reflect and ruminate in thought versus writing it

down as an alternative. Once this is complete and we feel a sense of satisfaction, closing our eyes in a room at a temperature that is cool/cold will probably lull us to sleep. Our minds are now clear and we have come down from cloud nine. Entering sleep can happen in a relaxed way.

Keeping a sleep log may add some logic to our less than restful nights. This may help monitor the mental and psychological factors effecting our sleep. We will next address the physical and spiritual factors that can be holding us back. Let's take a look at how Mitchell's mother handled his brother, Simon's, days or nights of running the streets, in the next fictional story.

The fictional story of Mitchell's brother Simon and their mother, follows here:

CHAPTER 8

A MOTHER'S MOUNTAIN MOVING FAITH

She had faith that which is strong enough to move a mountain. She had a wayward son, Simon, but she and her LORD and Savior Jesus Christ knew that at the appointed time, her son would come running back to Christ saying, "LORD, LORD, I repent and have fallen astray. What must I do to be saved?"

You see, her son's day didn't start until the wee hours of the night where he would engage in his unrighteous and illegal acts.

But his mother, his mother would stand firm on Jesus' words found in St Matthew 17:20 that reads: **"For truly I say to you, if you have faith like a grain of mustard seed, you will say to this mountain, move from here to there and it will move and nothing will be impossible for you."**

She would pray so deeply and earnestly for her son. She knew that the Word of God says the prayers of the righteous avail much. You see, she remembered that Paul wrote in 1 Thessalonians 5:17, **"Pray without ceasing"** and that's exactly what she did. Interceding for her son day and night, this mother got those "mountain moving" results.

Now Christmas fell on a Sunday that year. His mother being virtuous and bold, invited her son to church, confident he would attend. Ahh yes, I say she was confident. Her faith was strong and she didn't second guess that God would move on her son's heart the way only He can. I'm glad to say that on that Christmas day, her son Simon, gave his heart and life to Christ---

never returning to the streets or looking back like Lot's wife, but moving forward, worshipping, and serving God daily. As for his mother, she always knew in her heart that her labor and prayers would not fall void. God truly has the victory!

CHAPTER 9

DEEP THOUGHTS on A MOTHER'S MOUNTAIN MOVING FAITH:

Sleeplessness

Don't be afraid of it when it comes. It's not a sign that anything is wrong. God never commanded sleep in His account of Creation. He puts you into sleep just as he put Adam into a deep anesthetic sleep before He performed surgery on him and Eve was formed. When sleep doesn't come, notice how your body reacts while you stay awake beyond 16 hours. I notice that my digestive system goes kittywack and I begin to eliminate a lot, almost to the point of diarrhea.

The digestive system is delicate. After I had common abdominal surgery in a Caesarean birth, I noticed that my digestive system was the last thing to recover from the anesthesia. I had to have a catheter and a liquid diet. Too, a young human's digestive system isn't fully developed until years after birth, when the toddler is about 2 or 3 years old and is potty trained.

So, don't think it's strange that your body may react to your sleeplessness. Eat light when it happens. You don't want to stress your digestive system. Foods that I have found to lead to a restful sleep are oatmeal and pasta.

SLEEPLESSNESS & LONELINESS may have been around for decades, centuries, and millennia, but I believe it was heightened in America after the airplane bombing of the Twin Towers in New York City in 2001…marking the death of personal comfort for so

many. A sense of national uncertainty of life and liberty loomed over Americans as my heart sank for the love and loss of more than just lives and building structures. Confidence was lost… confidence in America, confidence in God, confidence in ourselves. For some, lives were turned in a tailspin topsy-turvy, with no way, idea, or solutions to get back to "normal". Some still haven't. The crushing of the spirit left a dark spot in the three places that we have a heart…head, chest, abdomen. If the dark spot is a spot and not a hole, then damage has been done. If the dark spot is a hole, then it can be mended, healed, then cured permanently. It is as if a mountain is in the way. Sleeping pills and Meet Up functions only offer temporary "fixes" whereas, **FAITH**, can move these kinds of mountains.

You don't have to be religious to have the kind of **FAITH** that I'm talking about. I'm talking about the acronym **F.A.I.T.H.** = **Fear Absent In The Heart.**

With all of my formal education and knowledge in neurology, neuroscience, neuropsychology, theology, neurospirituology, school-based & medical speech/language pathology and communication sciences/disorders, as well as being a business owner and leader; it has all culminated as a heart problem at the crux of sleeplessness & loneliness.

I'm not saying that all you need is faith and the wave of a magic wand to be free of sleeplessness and loneliness. It will take some doing…soul-searching, self-discovery, and copious amounts of self-love, shown in how one communicates & interacts with others and oneself. Keep reading for help.

CHAPTER 10

DEEP THOUGHTS ON SLEEPLESSNESS AND LONELINESS:

Love is the cure…permanent cure. Love gone wrong, is also the culprit. I can't say that this hypothesis has been tested and researched on a wide swath of participants. But I can say with emphatic emphasis that it is a driving source that can cure even if the love is not directed towards nor stemming from another individual. Self-love can cure sleeplessness and loneliness.

The characters, Mitchell and Lucille in the drama scenes in this book, have not always been married. They spent over a decade in life as singles. In that time, they chose to prepare themselves to meet that special someone who could bring out the best in them as they grew old together. The power of knowing who you are in and of yourself, as well as in relationship to the rest of the world, is the energy that powers self-love.

If you are looking for a step-by-step guide of tricks or miracles that you have not tried, out of the many attempts you have made to increase your sleep and feeling of social acceptance, you'll be once again disappointed.

Take note of the love that evolved between Mitchell and Lucille.

CHAPTER 11

LONELINESS

The drama continues:

After awhile, Mitch and his brothers got into an altercation that led to the remote isolation of the three. The drug addict, turned Christian Saint, became a dreamer. The stoic righteous one became crazed. However, Mitchell, realized his faults and was disgusted with them. He tore off the metaphoric heavy metal gold chain that once shined and showed off his prowess. But now it only left a crock in his neck. Seeking comfort to ease the metaphoric disease he had caught by hankering around with the wrong people in his lonely mind, and doing the popular Internet Web remedies for the past 5 years; his dying disease and disgust only progressed.

"ENOUGH" he shouted, raising his right hand and arm high, higher than ever with his rotator cuff torn and healed 7 years ago. Those days of isolation were lonely days for Mitch. He slept a lot at times and slept very little at other times. These days were very depressing for him. He missed his brothers and mother and never knew his father. But not too long after these days, he would find happiness in life and fullness in his heart.

CHAPTER 12

DEEP THOUGHTS on LONELINESS:

Through life's experiences in the life as the primary author, I had a successful career working with children for 30 years and adults for 14 years. It is my thought and vision given to my medical speech/language pathologist's Mensa-Mind, that God provides us the predestined success cells necessary to avoid sleeplessness and loneliness. These cells that I am suggesting, make up a gland in the human brain that is activated like the pituitary gland, which regulates the onset of puberty. When activated, this gland releases cells that increase one's self-love and self-friendship at specific times in one's life. When the individual makes the conscious and subconscious decision to organize their leisure time with options of productivity, this lets the Creator, God, know that that person loves him/herself enough to be that same person's friend; which is God's reason for creating each one of us. Then self-love and self-friendship are released…making them successful and compatible for marriage.

CHAPTER 13

A FATHER'S LOVE

The fictional story continues:

Mitch & Lucille came to this life-changing decision in their early 30s and it lasted till death did they part in their 90s. Their marriage was magical and they loved with Pure Love for self, God, and others.

When Mitchell died at age 97, Lucille was 93 and sleeplessness and loneliness tried to set in. But the photo albums that they saved, binders with achievement rewards, notes from their Bibles and religious books that they studied from together, served as physical evidence of the joy and happiness in her soul. When she viewed them and watched videos of their grandchildren, that zygote energy of self-love and self-friendship came back. Yes she was alone but not lonely. And yes, she had restful sleep. She loved herself, God, and others. She was her own best friend. The cells in her body provided spaces for her to think and reorganize her leisure time as well as sleep, eating, and exercise hygiene.

Lucille was active in the community and loved to pass on the story of Mitchell's love as a man, husband, and father. She and Mitch spent many years childless and happy until the internal clock started ticking loudly.

As the story is told, Mitchell was a man of great stature. His reputation among the greats in the city---and those to come before him and after, was found to be exquisite. This man's personality was admirable, sweet, and peppered with integrity and dignity---but most importantly, love. Almost everyone he encountered was left

with the impression, that he was an awesome man and there needsto be a replica of him. Everyone thought that it would behoove him to have a child---a son.

The dilemma was he married at age 34 and his wife never wanted kids. He was okay with that fact, but it didn't suppress his love for children.

Then years had passed and the couple were still together growing and sharing in love. With him now being at the age of 43 and her, his wife at 39---almost 40, they basically watched each other grow and mature for the better. There were still no, unexpected pregnancies. The coupled acquired a few businesses and made some wise investments over the years but yet and still...no offspring.

Though his wife was very firm in the beginning about not wanting children, she always knew that her husband would be a great father and she a good mother...she just really didn't want the responsibilities.

Faith was always key in their household. The couple became closer and stronger in their walk with God. They began reading the Bible more and getting along better with each other. They really were falling in love, respect, and honor all over again. Things were now so good between the two, it only made sense to give a baby...a child, an environment like that. They both thought about it, but hadn't yet verbalized it to each other. They both thought and this is after they remodeled their contemporary home, I might add, "ahhh this is nice but there's got to be more to life than this."

One day a friend of the family met with them and told them she adopted two boys---her sons. She was just elated over the joy she

found in them. They were 4 and 6 years old. She told them that they were a blessing from God and that one day the LORD is going to bless her with a husband. The couple spent the day with their friend, Emily, and they both realized that there was an element to life that they were missing because they were not parents, though they influenced many youths. Emily's sons were so loving and full of life, it was a true pleasure for them to be around them.

When the couple got home, Lucille said, "You know that was a real selfless act for Emily to adopt those boys." Mitch said, "I know, and you and I have the perfect situation for that because we aremarried." Lucille said, "I know, but we are getting up in age." "I know", said Mitch. The subject was then dropped.

Though Lucille didn't really want to…she couldn't stop thinking about Emily and her two adopted sons and even her and Mitch having a child even at their age.

When Mitch came home from work, Lucille discussed with him not using contraceptives anymore. She said they'll take it as it comes if they get pregnant…well if it happens, it happens. To Lucille's surprise, when she said that, he picked her up and spun her around, kissed her, and said, "Thank you Baby, cause I was thinking the exact same thing!!"

Three months later, Lucille was having stomach issues, went to the doctor and…you guessed it! Lucille & Mitch were pregnant. Mitch was so excited when she told him!! He was there for her for the whole pregnancy. He decorated the housed and added a "baby wing". Preparation after preparation, nine months later they had a beautiful baby boy, Mitchell Zachary Carson, Jr., was finally here.

Mitch senior was led to journal his thoughts of what it means to be a father in the latter years of his life. He told God it gave him great and immense joy that God blessed him and Lucille with their new bundle of joy even in his late 40s. Mitch prayed that God would keep him alive, young, and fit so that he could enjoy the years of their son's life. He said he felt like Abraham in the Bible who had a baby with his wife at 100 years of age!!! And as things would turn out, they had a baby girl a year and a half later.

And let's not forget to mention Lucille and her gratitude, for she was almost certain she would never be a Mom. But she allowed God to soften her heart and she couldn't be all the merrier. Mitch loved their son and daughter. There's nothing like a father's love.

Mitch and Lucille raised their kids in the LORD. From changing diapers to soccer games, to of course Sunday School and church.

Mitch was teaching his son how to be a man, and Lucille was teaching their daughter how to be a lady. It was all worth it…a welcomed venture and experience they never forgot. Mitch Senior taught their son football and baseball, and basketball. They raised their children to be upright, respectable, and just. Emily even met a man and married. So, the two families always fellowshipped with each other and had dinner and other family activities together.

Since the couple had made some wise investments in the earlier part of their marriage, they had enough money to put their son and daughter through college. Mitch Junior studied Information Science with a minor in Music. So did their daughter. Mitch Senior and Lucille were so proud of them. They were now in their 70s. The children married and had daughters. Mitch Senior and Lucille were now grandparents.

What a change of events. They didn't plan for it, worked hard to go against it, but thanks be to God, they have children of their own and grandchildren now!

Sometimes in life, the thing you never want to happen ends up happening anyway and it's one of the best things that could have ever happened to you!!

CHAPTER 14

DEEP THOUGHTS on SPACES THE BOOK:

Self-love and self-friendship lead, in my experience, to automatic servosystem bodily balance, known as homeostasis. Take the stories and Deep Thoughts of this book and shift your mindset to address your sleeplessness and/or loneliness, or that of a loved one.

No one will ever have a one-size fits all answer to loneliness and sleeplessness. In Genesis chapter 2, God solved both of these problems in biblical Adam, with the making of his wife Eve. God said it is not good for man to be alone, and made a help meet after putting Adam in a deep sleep.

This book's look at both loneliness and sleeplessness, from a neurospirituologist, can give the reader a fresh look at these ills from a point of view that takes into account the physical, mental, and spiritual holistic aspects, with the curative outlook that was afforded biblical Adam. Adam lived to be over 900 years old and probably told God at that time, that he was ready to step into Heaven's Eternity, and God granted him that…his death.

It is with my regret, the primary author, that I did not address per se, the loneliness and sleeplessness of life-long unmarried people with little hope of finding a mate. But let them have the Peace that I achieved at age 12, knowing in my soul that my soul was of the marrying type. Marriage did not come until age 36. Divorce came at age 41. Failed hopes that the divorce would reverse lingered until age 52. New love was found and a happy marriage happened at age 57. Loneliness was never a part of my life and sleeplessness was never constant.

This book offers new ideas that may open the reader's mind to personal peace not addressed within the pages of this book, but offers enlightenment towards an end of loneliness and sleeplessness.

The idea of this book began in the 1980s when God gave the primary author, a neurospirituologist, a vision. The vision was a pioneering vision of brain cells. The Divine Vision occurred while she was working on her Master's degree where she excelled in the area of the Central Nervous System. As she evolved, so did the inspiration to write a book on these cells in the brain, which are related to loneliness and sleeplessness.

With its unique design, the coauthor's drama passages, lace the deep thoughts of the primary author, with vivid and entertaining literature that will home in the essential points that seek to bring understanding.

Please know that both authors feel for those who suffer from loneliness and sleeplessness, and wish all the best for those led to benefit from this book. God Bless You.

www.ingramcontent.com/pod-product-compliance
Lightning Source LLC
Chambersburg PA
BHW051240120626
547CB00014B/1730